vodka-mountain

Kelly Sexton

vodka-mountain©2017 by Kelly Sexton. Published in the United States by Vegetarian Alcoholic Press. No part of this work may be reproduced without expressed written consent of the author. For more information, contact vegalpress@gmail.com

always
7
folding
8
grand irish envy and a weak long fix
9
beer tastes like shit
10
not responsible for lost or damaged egos
11
paying to be primal
12
thick noise of a carpeted brick building
13
visitation
14
mushroom-tomato omelets and a weak long fix
15
a day in the life of charlie the chimp
16
post regeneration
17
'..'
18
drinking unidentified white wine
19
done
20
nebraska, home of arbor day [oh-my-huh?]
21
gorge-us on death
22

chrono-logical
23
darkened milk-sun
24
how dare you fill my void
25
poem pretending to read itself
26
if i could make it so...i would make it slow
27
stop whistling, it's making me nauseous
28
sweaters on, windows down
29
cold fettuccini alfredo
30
monday awakening
after Ken McCullough's Sunday Nap
31
I-IV
32
the bloody birth of word
35
schatzie
36
empathy
37
different title
38
wet napkins
39
i'm standing in piss right now
40

...
41
starin' at aaron
42
where's your hat?
43
title me-i'm lonely
44
memoirs of a disgruntled pet
45
beautiful blue bullshit
46
this weak text represents my day
47
the carnations instead
48
sad salamander cleans the bowl
49
form
50
into the ( )
51
glassed over
52
past tense
53
3.0
54
revisiting the ellipses era
55

november
56
february
57
closing the tab
58
newcastle
60
rosario filtro
62
recruiting
63
teaching
64
when i become an artist
65
abandoning
66
quickening
68
the woulds
69
steal this line
70
appropriately strong title
72
committed
73
to keep in your wet pocket
74

vodka-mountain

always

we could live on a piece of land
in the middle of

and we could have a fountain
next to the

and my subjective reality
is superior to

but the only problem is
with the fountain of

because, even with signs
someone always pisses in the fountain

folding

when you sleep i disappear
crumple into my head and
leak on the pillow for hours

vacant sanctuary,
dried out anointment

it's not hard to be alone,
it's hard to realize
how long you've been that way

grand irish envy and a week long fix

i am you

when you are lonely
i'm still there
mothering your pain
holding your dirty rapture

you are not what they've made you
i can see that
even though i'm blind

your thoughts fall on my fists
melt turrets of truth on dry soil

they're all in the dark,
they all want to be.

beer tastes like shit

like vomit if you get a good one

why do you always need a backup beer?
because i need one close by in case i have liver failure,
i'll need something to slam before i go to the hospital

no open bar at the ER you know

culturally constructed coping mechanism
the yeast beast and a foul odor from the depths of
his belly

he teaches me with his grin
that is only half in
this world

he lets me learn from his logic, so crass
what i've always sensed to be true

choose to be blue-collar,
don't become part of their shit

don't even look at it

not responsible for lost or damaged egos

wrought with the emptiness of silence

broken hedonist

you will lose me
as you have lost
all in your life

without regret.

an empty threat
waiting to be filled

paying to be primal

i'm a bad camper
that wears socks all the time
with organic bug spray
citronella underwear

i start fires with lighter fluid
not logic
and burn like a thin skinned
daughter of whales

maybe i'm bad at camping
because i'm bad at living
or haven't been doing it long enough
to see that i have more to learn
from every lost beginning
i've ignored

i've always thought of butterflies as weak and fluffy
they're more like tiny frat boys with wings
flying with the chaotic texture of a DUI
and opening the already-opened gifts of the flower

maybe i'm a good camper;
fuck you

thick noise of a carpeted brick building

i saw a cop give a kid his first underage drinking ticket tonight
it was sad and there's no other word
he read his ticket out loud then leaned against the cop car
crying
no, please, i don't have this kind of money, you don't understand
the cop responded, *get off the car*
so he leaned there with his crushed forehead on the window.

it would have been horrible to see what his face looked like at that moment
smeared with fear and young shadows.

blood on glass distorts human recognition.

get off the car, the cop announced again.
when he drove off the kid ran after the car for a few feet
then collapsed in the alley.

i closed the curtain and thought
about desperate nights of explanation
and hollowness in my belly.

anxious sweat
twisting the marrow and guilt that holds life together
for one
more
hour.

visitation

been a long time
shaking now
paying more attention to the shadow of the movement of my hand
than these words
revision will need to wait…
forever.

keep wanting to yawn but afraid i'll open too wide and my jaw will fall off.

just because something is moving
doesn't mean it's alive.

no new messages.

mushroom-tomato omelets and a weak-long fix

you can slit your wrists with this pen
a thousand lifetimes at a time

this isn't what i ordered

your empty words fall on neurons
that refuse to fire
move the impact aside
manipulate the lactic acid
to the lips

w-o-r-k f-o-r i-t

fuck all of it
the self
all that you have created
re-created

folding chairs that never collapse
and a desire for the lack of lust
make my existence w-holy
fall beneath my rubble

submit to the weak hands that paw at strings
and the "drummer" posturing to keep up with licks

i think of bald spots and how
i hate sympathy
and how i love to give it away
like candy
like scowls

several pumps of the valve
and lost ownership of the left ventricle

a day in the life of charlie the chimp

you think that animals will have
some reaction to the sound of a voice
the stare of grey eyes
the funny look of text

charlie doesn't know me
glances past my bleeding eyes
to a friendlier chimp with fat hands

expectation is a browning poison
that sits and moans in the corner for more

post regeneration

when the world stops for those seconds at a time
i can feel the suffering…usually not my own…
the horror…
and conrad crying to his page…
the turned belly of a rat…
and tears pour…
and all i ever do is petition them to stop…

and my article has been PR-ed…
again…
maybe i should be glad that important white men [with secretary-cum-stained sleeves]…
decided to cut the minimum-waged intern out of the budget…

but fuck it…

i eat unwashed apples…
i eat pills that make my head right…

just don't like getting PR-ed…
or the strap-ons my lawyer used on the poodle all those years…

`\_/`

other animals don't kill themselves
they just give up on living
lie down on their snouts in the mud
let the world swallow them
cut and broken from eternal existence

there is no two
only one and one
it is
or
it isn't
and
it isn't

drinking unidentified white wine

and pawing at my awkward notebook
re-experiencing the willow that never weeps
and
the sloping roof of my bare toes

fall from earth
wrap your hair around the thinning skull

done

i don't smoke cigarettes or play guitar
i hate beer and
i can't read this

it must be beautiful

nebraska, home of arbor day [oh-my-huh?]

for the purposes of easy travel i find myself in nebraska
wondering how cheap the housing would have to be to keep
someone here

omaha has five lanes to nowhere with stubby lights
which i presume are tractor headlights or denny's parking lots
stuffed with college toys

people of nebraska come find me
take your exit
448 is great?
are pharmaceutical sales higher here
mmm...pfizer
when will i stop being a sad raindrop?
can *you* tell me T.V.?

gorge-us on death

when a child asks me why do lightning bugs glow
i say they're magic because i don't know either
an adult is a child that knows it's a child

the bug hit my windshield, broke apart
his light separated from the dark body
stayed glowing
death gave light, glowed long after
made hostages of my eyes

separate my glowing stomach from the dark portions
stay lit
even after flesh has been abandoned
after light leaves grey eyes

chrono-logical

to miss what you do not know
and move from familiar ground
for the berry
crushed as you bite at the side

and even if you are just the open
gesture to an empty sky
[that i suspect you are]
i will welcome your eyes

the waiting can stop
as the brain can fail

and i will consume
what's left of your veil

my body still churns
with the rot of the you--
old
age

loss and hurt
won't dissipate

please come find me
in my library of tears

show me the way

it's been too many years.

darkened milk-sun

i like to pretend the generic moon is ours
that it has cried dry again
slouching by the dull throb of the stars that cry backup
eyeballs sliding back to their cups
material distanced, skewed
hard to hold in little white fists at bedtime

fall down on these beeswax-stained thoughts
watch as the pressure folds in
and all that you love become angels of dust
lost in nonmemory and icons of the past

and always the watery eyes
and always the ballpoint nothingness

waxing
waning
waiting

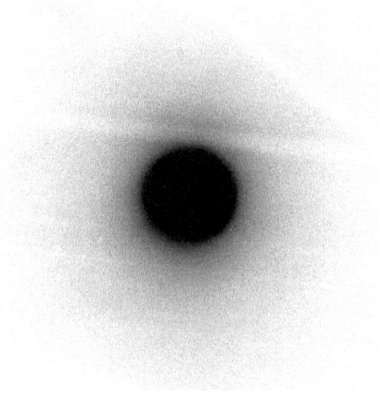

how dare you fill my void

thoughts still scalding my brain, they will not retreat
now i beg for sleep every moment i'm awake
and i beg for drink
and i beg for your touch one more time

i can smell your somber heart through the stink of sulfur in this town

stop reading this and drink

poem pretending to read itself

tonight i will read to a crowd full of strangers
and i will wait with an even heavier heart
regretting that i left you for *all of this*

if i could make it so…i would make it slow

make me weak, watch me fall
your hands on me were never cold
your body wrapped in fine light
a nerve recoated, refastened onto swollen muscles
i imagine you old and in pajamas
with a bowl of cereal in one hand
and a folded left around your ribs
grappling at what i can't stop touching

yet enter the forced negation
the pursuit of the logic
the snuffing of the fire
the attempt to bully my heart
scowling at myself

stop whistling, it's making me nauseous

let's play pool at another bar
i prefer to lose in unfamiliar surroundings
you will be smothered over
suburban excrement on converse shoes

charcoal lines thrown on paper to mimic your perfect form
waiting at the foot of the door without shoes
never begging for admittance
a chaotic ear with angular impatience
bar drivel and the lost moments i beg for

my humanity is as flawed as your sense of humor
my ability to accept as wounded as your ego

rid the self of the judgment you call intuition

lay down

sweaters on, windows down

cat becomes a sort of illegal muffler, envelops the beginning
on close smooth light
lies, unraveling, delinquency
loss forces covens
stops all equilibrium, guttural scream of a child
hands pervading love
perpendicular to nothing
the other fallen fortress (now just undress)
below, openings last
darkened, dorsal, not deterred
fallen, unrevised
never careless, stagnate tents of grammatical death
sketch off smoke
ignore the backs of throats, take-a-bite

cold fettuccini alfredo

are you upset with me?
should have been countered with
are you fucking retarded?

maybe next we can fight over coasters
or drapes
or nothing at all

we could debate the history of the handgun
or i could hand you the comics
and you could pretend to read

time is better spent on angry poems
than hanging on the words of a child

i could be plagiarizing right now
or forgetting my name

which
-
it seems
-
i've already done

monday awakening
after Ken McCullough's Sunday Nap

i wake up at noon and remember it
is the last day of our relationship
that i now must walk forward
through the truth
to leave you here

I

still can't find the words...
just the drink...
don't want to see choi like this...
don't want to see...
showering was a chore...
sitting here right now is a chore...
over-obsession with seeming theme of this existence...
being focused upon the questioning of whether or not one should be...

II

i looked through the trees to see our waning moon...
i thought about how you had failed me...
realizing i had only failed myself...
with cornerstone-soaked gazes past you...
alprazolam-induced ignorance...
with authoritative paranoia...
glued to keyboard...
anxious fits of disbelief...
ending transmission...

III

high cheekbones...
long-faced revelations...
i look at you now in pictures
and feel like i should have seen it in your eyes...
knowing...or thinking...
that you were so much like me
that you would somehow, by luck, find shallow water
just for a moment...
find the breath to keep you alive
one more night
until the events of the next day
could distract you...

IV

i gnaw on the memory of everyone holding your body up in that box and thrusting to hearse your vacant sanctuary...
the nightmares will not end...
and, believe, although there is no horror, they are indeed nightmares...
no dreams would tease me with your existence the way these do...
and will...

light of angry youth faded to a stub
faculties shut down
sensory deprivation one step at a time
and swallowed like brine shrimp
by a devouring loneliness

everything is emptied
the world splits open
presents its belly for you to scratch
and the bark burns to steel
what the earth cannot own

horse pills of truth tear up the inside
and run blood trails down the middle of the country

and his face has become a headstone reminder

that wrapped his body around that gun

tip in mouth
toe on trigger
melting from the top

four walls, no door
no ceiling, no floor

the bloody birth of word

was it wrong of me
to want to see you lying
open like the curling
end of a petal

my limp fingers
lying on the concrete
next to the machine
that types my life away
holds my beautiful lies
gives me nothing but the relief
that i can fall asleep
now that the pain has left my head
and stained my page

why is creation so painful
why is what is painful so
absolutely gorgeous

i believe in free publications now
come sit with me for a whole day
a whole day of white wall and rolling marble
i will type and bind you up a chapbook

i will sit with you in silence

schatzie

when hateful words drop on my mother
i think of how she was your baby

each night i visit you
even though you died
years ago
in the sunroom
under the weight
of your clammy hands
on your weakened chest

and i walk through your house
in the corner of my mind
so that i won't ever forget
the steps you took
over thick rugs
past an out of tune piano
to your garden

when i drink whiskey
i drink it for you

and when i smell the oil
of my face after hours
of work and days without shower
i smell you

these parts of you i keep
harbor them for the world

harbor them from the world

that you left me in

empathy

the second half of every life is spent trying to relive the first

can't find the
can't feel the
don't want the

reject

long process of elimination
ending with the loss of molecules,
deterioration of matter

doesn't matter.

you don't look truth right in the eye
you don't deviate from the money goal
you don't fast for anything
you don't feel for anyone

and it sets every element on fire at once
and it bursts inward to swallow hollow thoughts
and it eats and devours the world you thought you owned

and i want to be

but i don't believe

different title

each eye has become a smaller version of myself
vomiting tears after an evening of life

take away this subjective
let me be
hold my hair
sift the hurt
and
roll the loss into
the delicacy it has become
to my blackened tongue

i will see you in my mind forever
behind the dead third eye
because
that is the only place
you can be found

i'm not lazy
i've just given up

and i can't decide if david should wait
at the edge of the water for his friends to walk out unharmed
or if he should walk in to meet them

wet napkins

the things i say compromise my job
and make me want to rip holes in my skirt
and burn christmas sweaters under heavy lamps

i find myself crying in the bathroom
holding the hand of my selfish *depression*
and holding the neck of a child never born

i have respect only for the trees now
my grey matter marbled with fungus
my best friends locked in their rooms

i don't want this
take it back

give me my womb

i'm standing in piss right now

the monkeys are dead
tell the chimps
they will weep for days
as will i

...

fragmented dead pen

and all i want is
your face close to mine
so i can feel the lost waves
i forgot to thank you for

my fucking mind is melting
my mind is melting fucking

and all i need is
your nothing-once more
the unloaded gun of disappointment
and the last line

starin' at aaron

i can see you right now, mr. sadface
with the kitty-cam on your nonexistent pussy

don't be sad
fake it for me

fast moving particles that forced the mania downward
if i was the one living in a box in your building
i'd watch those samurai movies with you and
make you scorched gingerbread

if it makes you feel better
right now
there's a battle in my intestine
the tofu is soaking up the tequila
and making rude remarks
about your mother

i think i just shit my pants

where's your hat?

in the earthy pit of your hand
you can find these claims:

the green is too dry

i have a case of the crazies
and
my fingernails are heavy with brandy

the flame has dried itself
under loose threads of light
and
there is a need that i do not recognize
going unfulfilled in a box under ornaments
and
the dog can't hear itself think
under tall conversation

in the earthy pit of your mind
you can find no water
but
you can be flooded out
at the drop of a hat

title me-i'm lonely

i'm sorry it hurts to see you happy
but i'm a bitch

brake-lines severed
he'll go further than expected

and the still-chained prisoner
runs faster than olympians

he>wants>it<more

now, a long neck
for the guillotine drinking...
previously soothing

her>hurts<with<violets

the air is softer than before
forcing stoic faces on pale light
continually maneuvering

the>desire<must<die

memoirs of a disgruntled pet

10:04
there was a man here...again
he tried to pet me
she went to bed without feeding me

01:05
she didn't feed me...again
i pissed on her blue bath mat
it'll take five showers for her to notice

13:15
i vomited foam today...again
that man wants me fixed
i pissed in his shoes an hour before he left for work
because *i've* still got some balls

03:07
she came home drunk...again
remembered to feed me, but spilled my water
not noticing i'd managed to remove my collar

15:21
the house reeks of weed...again
she laughed at me when i fell off the counter
her birth control is now buried in my litter box

beautiful blue bullshit

eyes small, weak
wet with nothing

mind pressing against
acoustic hatred
your smell
my desire

pulsating
electrical
internal
to
external

this weak text represents my day

bloated with fear and lack-of-wine
fat hands grabbing at small waists
the smell of ammonia and vomit
still lingering from the bowl

the flies puff up with yeasty eyes
and dart in-between frothing bodies
that wait for sex and drink
ride bunnies bareback

blue lamps leak lava
there is nothing psychedelic about it
moving sheets with the death stains of father
dampening oily teeth with the 18%

fleshy collisions cause uninvited life
find-your-part
pick through the leftovers and make your meal
show only that impossible to conceal

the carnations instead

stop reading and drink
have too many things spilled on you?
ask liz for the bar rag
and a shot
she already knows what you want
just say yes, please

hot tears standing in line behind the rage
bloody-mouthed sweet and sour children
that rampage the streets of our lost minds
folding in on fermented thoughts
of your sentimental noise

my words lack color
have monotone eyes
reference the truth
that i fail to touch

sad salamander cleans the bowl

after a mourning vomit and prayer to the nothing in his belly
sad salamander reaches for his skinny towel
he'd like to believe that it was a fungal rag
but hasn't the strength for the melodramatic

the earth penetrates his almost nonexistent heart
into bits of sad salamander debris
his intestines cramp with the bad eggs
of a well-done house fly

pressed to the back of his cloudy aquarium
there will be no freedom today
just hours of wait and playing with his own shit
…again

where is that thing?
the one that feeds him
makes squeals at the bottom
of the evening to his
vacant sanctuary

form

desperately pawing at beauty as it escapes…
begging for blankets on cold nights…
diseased mind…opened
sprawled across carpet

hands on hands
waiting, thinning
painting each other's naked bodies
strawberry vines winding to sky

your flesh was my nature
your eyes my lake by tent

into the ( )

there is want in my closed pillow eyes this night
and I wonder whose bed you're in
and I wish it were mine
and I wonder what your words mean
even to you

gushing finally scabbing over
waiting for pick
hoping for gauze

pulling at hair on backs of necks
holding my drink hostage
one more night

glassed over

i can smell myself through this hoodie and i beg for my body to end
the tips of my fingers are numb…the tips of my neurons refusing life
wait for it.
when this ends there will be no gratifying release
i watch for the moment the DMT will flow
hope is a four-letter word
i've been broken too long to be fixed
abandoned in the factory
looking blankly through
locked
glass
doors

past tense

when i tell a story about you
i still can't hear myself use that tense
he has red hair
not
        had
he is my friend
not
        was

reality yawns and breathes hot and cold
all over my face
and this slowing time falls
and my blood is still in my body
and yours is still on your floor

3.0

seeing you bleed is worse than my own cuts
i want to hold your head and tell you it's ok
but it's not
and it won't be
just bittersweet moments of release
tensed up fists punching their own flesh
what remains is a stump
unable to recognize beauty
cradling the ugly counterparts in our church coats
falling down in strange beds

we all hold this dark secret from the world
we all wonder why we're the one left to see
and we wait and we try to pray
and for most there is nothing to pray to
and for most there is

grab at pill, sedate away
rethink, rebuild, remember
suns that drag themselves across the horizon
men that force their feet to the floor
the dead light that lies down for us
mushrooming into our dark realism

revisiting the ellipses era

pieces of heart float in toilet…
what the ice-cream scooper missed…
wet and throbbing in my chest cavity…
often i wish i would have walked further into ocean…
often i wish for things that can't be with me again…

november

splinter-under-nail | irritated excitement
headachy anxiety | grabbing at words
one hand intrusive | touching everything on me
the other pensive | touching everything but me
moving close enough for response
hands fold and shake over each other
slide down greasy nose
fall to warm lap | continuing inaction
submitting to warmed gun

never knowing the smell of a hospital or the feel of iodine to arm
tasting beer then blood as last sensations
sitting outside the classroom where teacher has forgotten you

and from the grey mouth a melody

february

desperately pawing at beauty as it escapes
begging for blankets on cold nights
diseased mind…opened
body across carpet
broken from time
shell next to blood-soaked pillow
dead feet | boots still attached
stillness of eyes and chest

hands on hands
waiting, thinning
painting each other's naked bodies
strawberry vines winding to sky
holding ruins to chest

we sleep for the impossible
sit like a mountain dog
sedate what binds
no covering or chemical
no view or immense gatekeeper
open mouths become maps

your flesh was my nature
your eyes my lake by tent

closing the tab

i hear the cat in the other room
stomping around angrily at my non-attention
when his foot hits something hard enough
i think of you
and hope you decided you didn't want to sleep without me
that you drove back to town planning to break into my bed
that you abandoned her as you will abandon me

and i'm pissed
at myself
what is this jealous sadness in my belly?
and you ate all my tums.
my thoughts are rapid and hot
coursing through tight blood vessels
in my small head on this large, empty pillow
that sits waiting for your smell
it's 4 a.m.

eyes salty-hot again
there won't be much more of this
and i can drink you away

like my dead friend and the gaping holes love has left

newcastle

in what used to be your den
there were recovered bar stools
bitchy women talking with fat mouths
and
all the signs that would lead to you
on any other night tears sat on deck

in what used to be your den
there were new shots with new names
songs you hated pouring from the jukebox
and
conversation with ruptured heroin balloons
hiding in the intestines of abandoned dogs

in what used to be your den
there were sweaty jocks rubbing themselves
itchy homeless men picking up old drinks
and
willingly disgraced barflies
laying sideways on the metal runner

in what used to be your den
i imagined your slender corpse
sliding to the top of the soil

and
finding your way
back to the nest you started

throw your basket out
there were no eggs to begin with

rosarito filtro

reminds me of my dirty bathtub
which isn't to say i don't like it

but corners of mind
are what need the washing
in thin cotton on porch

three heads of three cops
found this morning
bodies four towns away

illegals crawl under tape
and sweat on leg contours

smuggled across border
in wet panties

wastes migrating from every cell
nucleus collapse |release-needs|

the fat man half-covered in garbage bag
will be the meat at your white table

and you will shit him out
as quickly as he was devoured

recruiting

so i do, against my will.

form clinging to formless
waiting to be fed

and
asato ma sat gamaya
or something to hold between teeth

falstaff, come back to the bar
i will pay your tab
buy you a shot of crown
laugh at your juvenile jokes

the cliché blood on your hands will be real
the spot *won't* come out
realize what your leader has forced you into
realize how you were wronged
and remember, and remember, and remember

teaching

the red plague rid you for learning me your language

this language that you gave me
i now use to devour your mouth
word-by-word | again-and-again

i've longed to destroy your reign
as long as i can remember
to release myself from your mangled hands

i will bite with these teeth
you helped me grow in my cave
and i will mop your blood with
the tangled hair of your only child
that i've found upside down
more than daddy wants to believe

no song will play
as i feed on your mistake
and leave you with the tears of others

your cruel destiny at my hands
isn't the suffering you'd like to imagine
but will be watching in stadium seats
as all you love suffer for you

when i become an artist

you want to be the hamster in the plastic ball

this noun is a metaphor

and this metaphor is a metaphor

the reflective surfaces allow you to contort

dimension-sphere without biology or broomsticks

shedding the burden that the imagination holds

setting heavy determinates

icicles melting, trembling above victims

waiting for fall

abandoning

the hot passion of distempered blood

quick to react with heart on hip
clinging to ball and socket
while the old forget the pangs
and wish for attention like this
              and this

time heals nothing under
the grow lamps of desire
or waiting to spore in dark corners
or flower for the cave
              far from home

throbbing under hand
just one time more
so that something will exist
only to remind you
what you will never have again
waiting for death

shortened breaths arrive late
bang on doors at night
show up unannounced
drunk on the couch
with distempered blood on face

quickening

*so at his bloody view her eyes are fled
into the deep dark cabins of her head*

jealous love grazed by red eyes
and
lost lips that bleed the dead juice of iambs

hold the remnants in undone arms
and
force what resists to bind tighter

shallow benefit of infatuation
and
my chemistry betrays me again

pull your eyes up from the pavement
and
pretend it's now
not then

the woulds

locked nature
sunken to grade
the cure is not good enough

feral children
with fogged-over eyes
crawl on all fours
bend like grass

grab mom's dress
hide behind
under table
under cover
under ground

give anything
to be loved
to be pure
to be well

steal this line

great opening
I especially like meta (?) lines like "the first stanza"…in the first stanza
move television line down

the first three lines are great
but less self-referential than the others

the little stanza that could
more wierd lines

maybe
-
add
-
breaks
-
into
-
here

can ya put a   space
here or something?

Take this out so this is right after this

I feel like these lines are half-cannibalized
I wonder what full cannibalization would look like

maybe I should be more careful with what I put on here
makes me question what I write on your papers, I mean poems

this poem has nice flow

I love the contrast between these two stanzas

Maybe consider writing a poem (or using this one)
With comments as part of the poem

While I like the last line it might be interesting
To end with the image of the sandwich

appropriately strong title

The moon doesn't give a fuck
about us
Great opening
Set up for deception
Maybe add some more
between these lines
The first stanza isn't doing all
it could

That's a rich juxtaposition
Great haiku
Interesting progression
Maybe more active verbs.
Less "ing"

There must have been
contextual issues

Take this out so this is right
after this

I feel like these lines are half-
cannibalized
I wonder what full
cannibalization would look
like

Everything works quite well
Besides the couple lines that
don't fit

While I like the last line it
might be interesting
To end with the image of the
sandwich

committed

everyone at this meeting is from new york
they talk about perry st.
and the meetings of the 70s
i try to ignore the 14 references to god

i watch him cry onto his lap
i put my hand on his leg
and realize we're not partnered as before
we're comrades that hold each other
through anxious tears and night sweats

my hands shake
i need a shower
the nausea ceased
stomach still shakes for food
though mouth has no interest

last night I felt my body
fold into his vulnerability
like a parasite he needed
temporarily to remove the disease
plucked away when the pain subsided

we are our own big brothers

reproducing ourselves
through mirrors
and useless rubbing
on useful mats

we become our own captors
in cages of purple envy

"welcome to chapter two," he says
and smiles

to keep in your wet pocket:

I'm terribly, horribly sorry if my lack of emotion and/or over-emotion caused any unwanted controversy last evening. Please do not take my behavior personally as I am a very angry/parched individual.

Thanks,
The Management

I'm terribly, horribly sorry if my lack of emotion and/or over-emotion caused any unwanted controversy last evening. Please do not take my behavior personally as I am a very angry/aloof individual.

Thanks,
The Management

I'm terribly, horribly sorry if my lack of emotion and/or over-emotion caused any unwanted controversy last evening. Please do not take my behavior personally as I am a very angry/disposable individual.

Thanks,
The Management

I'm terribly, horribly sorry if my lack of emotion and/or over-emotion caused any unwanted controversy last evening. Please do not take my behavior personally as I am a very angry/well-dressed individual.

Thanks,
The Management

I'm terribly, horribly sorry if my lack of emotion and/or over-emotion caused any unwanted controversy last evening. Please do not take my behavior personally as I am a very angry/pungent individual.

Thanks,
The Management

Kelly Sexton holds an MFA in Writing and Poetics from Naropa University, is the former poetry editor for *Bombay Gin*, and a lover of asparagus. She has been published in *Monkey Puzzle, Touchstone, Apothecary, Species,* and other journals and zines.